AI for Wildlife Management and Conservation

Tools and Techniques

Table of Contents

Chapter 1. Introduction

This Special Report delves into the fascinating junction where artificial intelligence (AI) and wildlife conservation meet, encapsulating a digestible exploration of complex, yet essential, technological tools and techniques. As a topic that might initially seem intricate, we've simplified the intricacies of AI, machine learning, and data analytics, demonstrating their power to propel the field of wildlife management and conservation forward. Whether you're an eco-activist, a technophile, or a curious soul seeking ideas to preserve our planet's diverse ecosystems, this report is designed to shed light on the remarkable impact AI can provide in this area. This journey will not intimidate you with dense jargon; instead, it will engage, enlighten and inspire you with real-life examples, case studies, and insights from leading experts. Get ready to embrace the refreshing blend of technology and nature, inspiring novel ways we can protect our planet using AI for wildlife management and conservation.

Chapter 2. The Intersection of AI and Wildlife Conservation

The concept of merging cutting-edge technology and wildlife conservation might seem worlds apart. Yet, as we delve deeper into our mission to preserve and protect Earth's diverse and irreplaceable wildlife, it becomes increasingly evident that technology, specifically artificial intelligence (AI), plays an essential role in realizing this goal. Artificial Intelligence has surfaced as one of the most promising tools in the fight against habitat destruction, biodiversity loss, and the increasingly surreptitious actions of wildlife traffickers. Using disruptive innovation as somewhat of a middle ground, AI helps us interface with the wild in novel ways that were previously unattainable.

2.1. Understanding Artificial Intelligence

Before we delve into the applications of AI in wildlife conservation, it is vital we have an understanding of what AI is and how it operates. Artificial Intelligence is a branch of computer science that equips machines with the ability to simulate human intelligence processes. This could mean learning from experiences, recognizing patterns, understanding complex data and making informed decisions. AI achieves these feats using differing strategies, such as machine learning and deep learning, both subsets of AI that enable machines to learn from experiences.

Machine learning provides computer systems the capability to automatically learn and improve performance without being explicitly programmed. It mostly specializes in processing, analyzing, and making predictions based on vast amounts of data. On the other hand, deep learning employs neural networks, built like the human brain, with several layers that process and understand input data progressively deeper.

Now let's explore how these novel technologies intersect with wildlife conservation.

2.2. Leveraging AI in Biodiversity Monitoring and Wildlife Tracking

The use of AI in wildlife conservation mirrors the broader global trend toward digital transformation. Real-time tracking of animals using GPS and sensor-based technologies, drone surveillance, and camera traps are a few avenues through which technology interfaces with wildlife management. These methods generate massive amounts of data that require robust and efficient processing mechanisms – and this is precisely where AI comes into play.

AI-powered tools can analyze these diverse datasets faster and more accurately than traditional methods. For instance, AI's ability to recognize patterns enables it to identify specific species through camera trap photos, reducing the manual labor necessity. An emblematic case is the Wildlife Picture Index (WPI), an AI-powered tool that processes millions of trap camera photos to recognize different species automatically.

AI also plays a critical role in predicting and mitigating human-wildlife conflict. By using AI to analyze existing data on animal migration patterns, we can predict areas where humans and wildlife are likely to come into conflict, such as farmlands or transport corridors. Such prediction capabilities help shape strategies to mitigate conflict.

2.3. AI-driven Anti-poaching and Anti-trafficking Measures

Poaching and wildlife trafficking have posed significant threats to global biodiversity, pushing numerous species towards extinction. Implementing AI can substantively enhance traditional anti-poaching and anti-trafficking measures.

Machine learning capabilities can help predict poaching activities based on historical data such as known poaching hotspots, times of the year when poaching is prevalent, and socioeconomic indicators. This predictive capability helps law enforcement focus resources, conduct proactive measures, and essentially dissuade poaching attempts.

Similarly, AI can be a potent tool in combating wildlife trafficking. By training AI systems with imagery and information about illegal wildlife products, digital platforms can automatically detect and flag these items, reducing the burden on law enforcement authorities.

2.4. AI in Habitat Conservation and Climate Change

Our changing climate poses numerous threats to wildlife, impacting their habitats and triggering drastic alterations in behavior and survival. AI can assist in conservation efforts by predicting future climate patterns, the impact of these patterns on specific species, and suggesting adaptive strategies.

Sophisticated algorithms that handle vast weather datasets can predict future climate scenarios with remarkable accuracy. Combining these predictions with species distribution models can show us potential shifts in habitats and guide conservation efforts.

2.5. The Way Forward

The intersection of AI and wildlife conservation empowers us to navigate a multitude of challenges that have hampered traditional conservation efforts. Nevertheless, like an uncharted path, it comes with its fair share of obstacles, such as the necessity of appropriately training AI to ensure its responsible and effective use. Despite these challenges, the promise that AI holds is immense, providing an impetus to strategize its systematic integration into wildlife conservation paradigms.

As the potential of AI continues to unfold, we must remain aware of the ethical implications that could arise from its misuse. Setting and adhering to stringent ethical guidelines is paramount in preserving the delicate balance between technology's benefits and the profound respect we owe to Earth's wildlife.

Integrating AI into wildlife conservation practices is about more than just applying latest technology - it reflects a wider shift in understanding and preserving our environment. It demands a transformative vision, one in which technology doesn't dominate nature, but rather presents a harmonious synergy enabling us to safeguard our planet's precious biodiversity. While the journey is complex, the marriage of AI and wildlife conservation presents a compelling narrative that inspires and invigorates, offering fertile ground for our shared mission—to protect, preserve, and cherish nature's inimitable splendors.

Chapter 3. The Importance of Data in Modern Wildlife Management

Data is the driving force behind many modern industries and functions - from finance and healthcare to education and transportation. In the realm of wildlife management, its importance is perhaps even more significant. The role of data in wildlife management has evolved substantially over the years, paralleling advancements in technology, and echoing louder calls for biodiversity conservation. Employing technology in data collection, processing, and analysis has enabled us to glean unprecedented insights about the animal kingdom and its interaction with the environment. These insights are instrumental in shaping various wildlife conservation initiatives and safeguarding our planet's ecosystems.

3.1. Data for Understanding Wildlife Habitat Use

Understanding the habitat use and spatial ecology of wildlife species is crucial to informing the development of effective wildlife conservation strategies. Satellite tracking technology and GPS-equipped animal collars allow researchers to collect large volumes of data about a species's geographical range, habitat preference, and movement patterns.

For example, scientists studying African elephants can use this data to understand the animals' use of the landscape and their movements relative to protected areas and human-dominated regions. This valuable information helps in making informed decisions about landscape management, protected area design, and human-wildlife conflict mitigation.

3.2. Data-driven Population Monitoring

Monitoring the population and demographic structure of a species is fundamental to assessing its conservation status. Modern wildlife management employs technologies like motion-activated camera traps, drones, and even acoustic sensors to gather extensive data on wildlife populations.

Machine learning algorithms can process this data, identifying and counting individuals, estimating gender ratios, and even ageing animals. This granular information about population dynamics and trends helps in forecasting population changes, identifying threats, and implementing timely interventions.

3.3. Incorporating Climate and Land-use Data

Along with direct observations of wildlife, data on weather patterns and land-use changes also play a vital role in modern wildlife management. Long-term meteorological data can help understand how climate change is likely to impact wildlife habitats. Similarly, remote sensing technology provides up-to-date land-use data, revealing human-centric changes like deforestation, urban development, and agricultural expansion.

Analyzing these datasets together offers a comprehensive picture of the shifting constraints on wildlife and directs resources and efforts toward the most threatened areas and species. This integrated approach safeguards the continuity and resilience of ecosystems against both natural changes and human-induced disruptions.

3.4. Enabling Citizen Science Contributions

The rise of citizen science is another testament to the power of data in wildlife management. Digital platforms enable interested individuals worldwide to contribute to data collection efforts. For instance, smartphone applications offer an easy way for people to submit wildlife observations or make nature-based measurements.

AI can also process this crowd-sourced data, removing errors, duplications, and irrelevant entries. The cleaned data can then be pooled into broader studies, leading to valuable insights that might have otherwise been missed or underrepresented.

3.5. Informing Policy and Action plans

Data also forms an essential part of policy-making and planning in wildlife management. Integrated databases housing years of research and monitoring data provide a factual basis for developing conservation laws, policies, and action plans.

Data visualisation tools can help communicate this information to stakeholders in an easily digestible format. This feature is invaluable in rallying support, achieving conservation goals, and maintaining transparency in the process.

3.6. Conclusion

In an era where data is touted as the new oil, it's clear that wildlife management has much to gain by harnessing it. Whether to better understand how wildlife uses the landscape, to monitor and predict population changes, factor in climate and land-use changes, enhance citizen science or inform better policy-making, data is inherently interwoven into effective wildlife conservation efforts.

By exploiting technological resources to maximize data's potential, we move closer to a world where wildlife management is sharper, more responsive, and precisely tailored to each species's unique needs and challenges. Harnessing this resource responsibly and innovatively, we can ensure that modern wildlife management remains an effective steward of the planet's precious biodiversity for generations to come.

Chapter 4. Shaping the Future of Conservation with Machine Learning

In an era where human activities leave an irreversible footprint on our ecosystems, new and effective tools are needed. They're essential for understanding biodiversity, predicting species population dynamics, and planning conservation strategies. This is where Machine Learning (ML), a branch of artificial intelligence, enters conservation efforts.

4.1. ML Basics and Its Importance

Machine learning is an AI technology that falls under the broader umbrella of Data Science. It designs algorithms capable of 'learning' from data, making improvements, and providing predictions. In terms of conservation, machine learning lends itself brilliantly.

Machine learning has the potential to revolutionize field studies and redraft conservation by building predictive models from large and complex data sets. Whether you're analyzing animal movement, habitat changes, or poaching activities, machine learning can distill high-dimensional data into informative patterns. Thus, it frees researchers from the arduous task of manually perusing massive datasets while giving them the power to make comprehensive, data-driven decisions about future initiatives.

4.2. Machine Learning in Action: Notable Deployments in the Field

ML applications are blooming across various conservation platforms.

This section heaps light on notable ML deployments where technology is playing its part in revitalizing the existence of numerous species.

- TrackAI, an initiative by WWF and FLIR Systems, develops thermal and infrared cameras combined with ML algorithms to detect and differentiate species. This technology assists in patrolling and monitoring biodiversity hotspots, often pinpointing poaching activities.

- Scientists at the National Oceanic and Atmospheric Administration have been using machine learning to track and count Alaskan fur seals from aerial images, exponentially increasing their counting accuracy and saving hundreds of hours of manual work.

- Wild Me, a non-profit tech organization, uses image recognition algorithms to identify individual animals from photographic surveys. The data are used to study animal populations, monitor their health, and ascertain long-term trends.

These pioneering deployments of ML not only assist in data extrapolation but also facilitate the organization of data collected from fieldwork into a digitized and simplified format, which is immensely beneficial for researchers.

4.3. Overcoming Conservation Challenges with Machine Learning

The power of machine learning doesn't stop at just analyzing data; it also empowers ecologists to convert this data into actions that catalyze effective and efficient conservation practices.

- Predictive Modeling: ML models can predict future ecosystem state based on current and past data. This ability assists immensely in the long-term planning of conservation measures and formulating disaster management plans.

- Precision Conservation: With machine learning, the process of conservation can become more precise and targeted, focusing resources on the most at-risk species and habitats.

- Anti-poaching Measures: Machine learning can also complement conventional anti-poaching techniques by predicting poaching activities through pattern recognition and enabling swift and targeted interventional actions.

- Understanding Species Behavior: Machine learning can dive into extensive animal data sets to create insightful behavioral models, helping researchers understand critical population dynamics like migration and breeding.

4.4. Future Visions: How Machine Learning can Shape Conservation in Coming Years

The augmentation of machine learning with conservation strategies has shown its potential in transforming the entire landscape of wildlife conservation, raising new hopes for a sustainable future.

Consider potential deployments of drone technology powered by machine learning algorithms. These drones could autonomously patrol protected wildlife areas, identifying and tracking animals, detecting human intruders, and assessing habitat conditions. Species distribution models could be created using large scale climate, geographical, and environmental data, leading to more efficient conservation planning.

Moreover, as more technology companies and conservation organizations join forces, we will witness the amalgamation of machine learning with Internet of Things (IoT) for decentralized data capture from various ecosystems. The resultant data proliferation will allow global stakeholders to partake in a monumental venture: creating a healthier and more sustainable planet.

In conclusion, while challenges persist, the joining of forces between AI, more specifically machine learning, and conservation underpins an exciting new era. These new technological advancements have started to reshape the landscape of conservation, allowing us to integrate efficient defensive measures to safeguard our planet's precious wildlife. The power of machine learning allows us to peek into the future, guiding our actions today for the prosperity of our ecosystems tomorrow.

Chapter 5. Powerful AI Tools Used in Wildlife Tracking and Monitoring

Keeping track of wildlife populations is a crucial task for conservation scientists. It helps us understand how animals interact with their environments, and guides us in our efforts to protect endangered species. Traditional monitoring methods, however, such as physical tagging or manual surveying, can be invasive and time-consuming. These constraints are being shattered by the advent of artificial intelligence, offering revolutionary possibilities for wildlife tracking and monitoring. Now, let's delve into the heart of AI-powered tools that are spearheading these transformations.

5.1. Using AI for Camera Trap Imaging

Cameras traps have long been employed in the conservation field to quietly capture images of wildlife in their natural habitat. The challenge until recently has been the ensuing task of processing these tens of thousands of pictures, usually done manually by researchers. Enter machine learning and data analytics.

Machine learning algorithms, specifically convolutional neural networks (CNNs), have been designed to identify different animals in camera trap images automatically. These systems can analyze thousands of images in a fraction of time it would take a human. Most importantly, they can identify the species, count the number of individuals, and even estimate their age and gender.

One example of such AI is the Wildlife Insights platform, a collaborative project involving several conservation organizations. A global database of camera trap images feeds the machine learning model, which gets refined continually, enhancing its capability to accurately identify varied species.

5.2. Radio Tagging with AI and Drone Technology

Radio-frequency identification (RFID) has been a staple of conservation technology for years. In recent times, these efforts are being bolstered using AI and drones.

Drones equipped with AI system can efficiently locate tagged animals over large tracts of land, cutting down on the time and resources spent on tracking. The AI enables the drone to interpret the RFID signals, identify the animal's exact location, and even assess immediate threats in the environment, such as poaching activity.

5.3. AI and Acoustic Monitoring

AI has also found a unique application in acoustic monitoring. Bioacoustic recording devices capture the sounds of the environment, which are then analyzed by AI systems capable of identifying specific species by their distinctive calls. They can distinguish and count individual animals within the species, thereby offering another method of population monitoring.

Cornell Lab of Ornithology's BirdNET is an excellent example of how effective these methods can be. This AI system can identify bird species by their songs, offering ornithologists an invaluable tool to survey bird populations on a large scale.

5.4. Satellite Imaging and AI

Satellite imaging has proven instrumental for wildlife monitoring -

especially for large and elusive animals. These images hold a wealth of information, yet extracting useful data used to be an incredibly laborious task. AI algorithms, like Google's TensorFlow, now allow for automatic identification of different species from these images.

For example, the PAWS (Protection Assistant for Wildlife Security) combines satellite imagery with machine learning techniques to predict poaching attacks. The algorithm has learned from past incidents' locations and times to predict where poachers might strike next, enabling preemptive actions.

5.5. DNA Metabarcoding and AI

Lastly, AI is also transforming the field of DNA Metabarcoding, an approach that involves analyzing environmental DNA (eDNA) samples to identify species in a given area. Machine learning algorithms can quickly sort through this data, categorizing the various DNA sequences into related species groupings.

In conclusion, the synergy of AI and wildlife conservation creates a potent mix of tools that can augment and refine our efforts to protect the diverse wildlife of our planet. These are not isolated paths but interconnected threads that celebrate the marriage of technology and conservation. As we forge ahead, there's no doubt we'll continue to discover novel ways in which AI can aid our quest to preserve and understand the natural world. The intersection of AI with wildlife tracking and monitoring demonstrates the immense transformative potential of this technology, and this is just the beginning. These successes are merely launching points for future endeavors and breakthroughs. In time, AI will continue to open doors, unmask new insights, and shape the future of wildlife conservation.

Chapter 6. Deep Learning for Species Identification and Population Estimation

Wildlife populations around the globe are subjected to ever-increasing challenges, ranging from habitat loss and climate change to poaching and disease. To help mitigate these threats, advanced surveillance and data collection mechanisms such as deep learning techniques have emerged as pioneering solutions. At its core, deep learning provides algorithms designed to mimic human-like decision-making, supporting indirect approaches to identify species types, estimate population sizes, and monitor habitats.

6.1. Leveraging Deep Learning for Species Identification

With the advancing capabilities of deep learning, species identification, which was a task primarily driven by human diligence and precision, is undergoing a significant technological evolution. The widespread adoption of image sensors and trail cameras has led to the accumulation of millions of images, culminating in large datasets. However, these datasets remain underutilized, trailing behind their potential, primarily due to the insurmountable task of manually sorting and analyzing such substantial volumes.

Deep learning offers a solution via convolutional neural networks (CNNs), a form of machine learning algorithm designed specifically for image analysis. CNNs can be trained to scan through these images and identify the species present, almost as accurately as a human could, but at a fraction of the labor cost and time.

Scientists have been using CNNs to sort through motion-sensor camera trap images to distinguish not only between different species but also between individual animals of the same species. A case study involves a joint venture by Microsoft and the San Diego Zoo, where they developed an AI model that can distinguish individual giraffes based on their unique spot patterns.

6.2. Case Study: Wildbook

Wildbook, a software framework that uses AI for photo identification of individual animals, is built around deep learning algorithms. The algorithm checks, compares, and contrasts the distinguishing features of a spotted animal (like a leopard) or the unique ridge patterns of a whale's tail, for instance. By uploading photos of these species shot from any corner of the world, conservationists can get unique insights on local population dynamics and track the migratory patterns of the species observed. The broader community of citizen scientists contributes pictures to the platform, enriching the data pool. Once the deep learning model is trained, the AI needs only seconds to perform what formerly required exhaustive manual labor.

6.3. Deep Learning for Population Estimation

Estimating the population of a species is a pivotal aspect of conservation efforts. Traditional methods can often be inaccurate and resource intensive, rendering routine monitoring impractical. Deep learning, however, enables population estimation accurately, efficiently, and non-intrusively.

Scientists have applied deep learning algorithms to gather population size information from wide-scale aerial images, drone footage, and satellite imagery. These techniques enable census operations that were previously impossible due to the inaccessibility of terrain or the vast size of the species' habitat.

6.4. Case Study: Seal Population Estimation

Researches at Duke University and the Island Ecology and Evolution Research Group used high-resolution satellite imagery and a deep learning model to count the population of Mediterranean monk seals, one of the world's most endangered marine mammals. The algorithm was trained to identify and count individual seals in the images, which were captured by satellite for non-invasive, wide-scale monitoring. This potentially groundbreaking use of technology, if adopted widely, could revolutionize the conservation efforts regarding endangered species around the globe.

In conclusion, the power, efficiency, and scalability of deep learning bring forth new possibilities for species identification and population estimation. As more data becomes available to train these algorithms, we can expect their accuracy to improve and their applications to expand, promising a profoundly enriched understanding of the world's ecosystems and the species they harbor. While challenges do exist, such as acquiring necessary high-quality datasets and interpreting complex results, the potential benefits these technologies offer towards protection and conservation of wildlife are indeed promising. The dynamic convergence of technology and ecology has truly entered an inspiring era, unveiling new hopes for the future of wildlife conservation.

Chapter 7. Predictive Analytics: Forecasting Threats to Biodiversity

Environmental change and human activity pose some of the greatest threats to wildlife on our planet, leading to unprecedented biodiversity losses. By predicting these threats, we stand a better chance at devising strategies to counter their impact, harnessing the immense predictive power of data analytics. The art of predictive analytics has revolutionized several fields, and wildlife conservation is just beginning to reap its benefits.

7.1. Predictive Analytics: An Introduction

Predictive analytics is a branch of advanced analytic techniques that forecast future outcomes based on historical data and analytic models. The insights derived from these predictions hold immense value for wildlife conservation, providing a potential predictor of where, when, and how threats to biodiversity might unfold in the future.

At its core, predictive analytics involves three essential steps:

1. Capturing and cleaning the data: All valuable predictive models start with quality data. In the conservation context, this could come from sources like satellite images, climate data, species population counts, or even local human activity data.

2. Building the model: Advanced statistical techniques such as regression analysis and machine learning algorithms are used to identify relationships within the data that can predict what might happen in the future.

3. Validating and refining the model: Once built, it's crucial to test how accurately the model forecasts outcomes. Over time, models are refined and adjusted as more data becomes available.

7.2. Predicting the Impact of Climate Change

A major threat for biodiversity in recent years is climate change. Fortunately, predictive analytics can model the likely responses of ecosystems and individual species under changing climatic conditions.

For instance, researchers predict migration patterns of species in response to global warming to preserve critical habitats. Scientists use Data-Driven Ecological Forecasting, a subset of predictive analytics, to analyze changes in ecosystems resulting from climatic transformations. The outcomes can support the design of resilient networks of protected areas that account for future climate-driven displacements.

7.3. Anticipating Human Interventions

Historically, most of the pressures on wildlife and biodiversity come from human activities, including deforestation, pollution, urbanization, and hunting. By analyzing patterns in historical data, predictive analytics can model the likely development trajectories and their associated impacts on biodiversity.

Predictive analytics facilitates spatial mapping of past and current human land use, enabling the anticipation of future human interventions that may be harmful to biodiversity. These spatial predictions can then inform land management decisions and conservation planning, helping design adaptive strategies that both accommodate human needs and prioritize biodiversity conservation.

7.4. Species Population Forecasting

Conservationists can leverage predictive analytics to monitor fluctuations in species populations and project how these may evolve over time. Predictive models build patterns and relationships from historical species population data and predict future populations based on these patterns. These predictive estimates are especially critical for endangered species, as they enable real-time management adaptations and inform proactive wildlife preservation measures.

By integrating various information—from environmental metrics and habitat changes to species-specific factors like reproduction rates, food availability, and mortality—predictive analytics has been used to inform management decisions for species ranging from African elephants to migratory birds.

7.5. The Future of Predictive Analytics in Biodiversity Conservation

Although the potential of predictive analytics in wildlife conservation is impressive, it's still in a nascent stage. The complex reality of ecosystems, climate change patterns, and human behavior offer many challenges that require continuous refinement of predictive models.

Predictive risk mapping can eventually aid in identifying "hotspots" of threats before they occur. Incorporating geospatial technologies like remote sensing and Geographical Information Systems (GIS) with predictive analytics could enhance wildlife monitoring and conservation efforts.

Further, predictions are likely to improve as we have more fine-grained data and improved algorithms. Interdisciplinary collaborations between conservation biologists, data scientists, local stakeholders, and policymakers can harness the power of predictive analytics to advance biodiversity conservation.

In a time where anthropogenic pressures and climate change pose substantial risks to biodiversity, predictive analytics emerges as a beacon of hope. Its potential application in wildlife conservation is a shining example of how technology can be employed to protect and preserve our world's irreplaceable wildlife. It's high time we dive deeper into this data-driven approach and unlock the potential of predictive analytics in the fight to conserve biodiversity.

Chapter 8. Drone Technology and AI: Aerial Surveillance for Wildlife Protection

Drones have evolved from novelty gadgets to crucial tools in various sectors, including wildlife conservation. Their ability to capture high-resolution images or videos, reach inaccessible areas, and operate at relatively low costs makes them perfect for several conservation applications. Nevertheless, the transformative potential of drone technology is fully realized when combined with the computational prowess of artificial intelligence (AI).

8.1. The Rise of Drones in Conservation

Over the past decade, drones or unmanned aerial vehicles (UAVs) have found a place in wildlife conservation efforts. Aerial surveillance provided by drones has been instrumental in population surveys, illegal activity detection, and habitat assessment. Moreover, drones offer unprecedented vantage points that can enable detailed aerial mapping and ecosystem analyses - something that was previously achievable only through expensive and resource-intensive means such as manned helicopter surveys.

AI integration has furthered the sophistication of drone use in the conservation space. High performing AI algorithms can process aerial images captured by drones in real-time, enabling immediate responses to threats or changes in the environment. For instance, algorithms can detect illegal logging or the presence of poachers, triggering rapid action.

8.2. AI-Enhanced Image Processing for Efficient Wildlife Monitoring

Drones equipped with AI-enhanced cameras can take wildlife monitoring to a higher level. These devices can capture continual video footage of vast terrains, including obscured or difficult-to-access areas. Advanced AI algorithms can automatically analyze these videos, recognizing and distinguishing different species.

By employing machine learning models, these systems can discern patterns over time, identifying anomalies that might indicate environmental stressors or changes in wildlife behavior. As the AI algorithms continuously refine their analysis and predictions over time, they facilitate informed decision-making, helping conservationists develop efficient, proactive strategies.

8.3. Drones and AI in Anti-Poaching Efforts

Predominantly in Africa, poaching continues to pose a significant threat to wildlife, driving species such as elephants, rhinoceros, and lions towards extinction. Traditional anti-poaching efforts involved manual patrols - a costly and risky endeavor. However, drones equipped with AI technology present a safer and more effective solution.

AI-powered drones are capable of conducting night patrols using infrared cameras. Machine learning algorithms can then analyze the footage in real-time to identify human figures, effectively cutting through the cover of darkness used by poachers. By immediately alerting park rangers with accurate location details, rapid and targeted responses can be actioned, significantly reducing the risk of animal loss.

8.4. Precision Conservation with Drones and AI

Precision conservation represents a new approach, focusing on high-resolution, site-specific information to deliver focused, resource-efficient interventions. Drones equipped with multispectral cameras, thermal sensors, and LiDAR (Light Detection and Ranging) sensors can capture a vast array of data. AI technology processes this data to generate accurate, detailed models of the habitat and the wildlife within it.

These models uncover insights about niche habitats and microclimates, helping conservationists implement species-specific and localized conservation strategies. This sophisticated understanding of the environment facilitates sustainable, effective practices, minimizing disruption to the ecosystem and promoting biodiversity.

8.5. Limitations and Ethical Considerations

While the advantages of drone technology incorporated with AI in wildlife conservation are significant, there are concerns that need addressing. Wildlife disturbances caused by the noise and presence of drones is one such issue. Moreover, the potential misuse of drones, such as in wildlife harassment or illegal hunting, necessitates clear usage guidelines and regulations.

The field of AI-aided conservation drone technology is, indeed, praiseworthy. As research and development continue, the future for drones and AI in conservation appears exceptionally promising: offering precise, efficient, and eco-friendly solutions to some of wildlife management's most pressing challenges. However, circumspect application, acknowledging ethical considerations, respecting wildlife, and prioritizing ecosystem integrity, is crucial to its continued benefit to wildlife protection.

Chapter 9. Use Cases: Success Stories of AI in Wildlife Conservation

There's an increasing awareness of just how pivotal AI technology has become in transforming the field of wildlife conservation. This chapter aims to delve into various exhilarating real-life examples and success stories of AI applications that have significantly advanced wildlife conservation.

9.1. AI for Animal Identification

One of the pivotal applications of AI in the field of wildlife conservation is facilitating animal identification. A prime instance of this can be seen in the successful project orchestrated by the Wildlife Conservation Society (WCS) and Google. Together, they have developed an AI system named "Wildlife Insights" which uses machine learning to identify individual animals based on their unique patterns and traits.

This AI tool has the ability to discern between different species - a vital feature considering the volume of image data typically collected in wildlife studies. It rapidly scans through countless images, successfully pinpointing unique characteristics of different animals. This initiates not only swift recognition of the species but also allows scientists to track individual animals across a specific geographical region, enhancing their ability to study movements, behavior patterns, and interactions within the animal community. It has proven instrumental, for instance, in monitoring species like jaguars and tapirs in South America.

9.2. AI for Illegal Wildlife Trade Monitoring

Illegal wildlife trading poses fatal threats to a vast number of species worldwide which are already racing extinction. AI is proving to be an indispensable tool in tackling this issue. TRAFFIC, an international wildlife trade monitoring network, has partnered with machine learning experts to develop an AI tool that identifies illegal wildlife products sold online.

Before AI intervention, this entailed painstakingly sifting through thousands of online ads manually. Now, the AI system scans these ads using image recognition and NLP (Natural Language Processing), identifying the ads that sell banned wildlife items and alerting the authorities. It's instrumental in disrupting the illegal trade and enhances the protection of threatened species.

9.3. Using AI to Predict Poaching Activities

Conservation Metrics and the USC Center for AI in Society devised an innovative approach to tackle wildlife poaching. They created an AI tool named "PAWS" (Protection Assistant for Wildlife Security), which utilizes predictive modeling to estimate the likely sites of future poaching attacks.

PAWS sources its algorithm from data generated from past poaching activities and patrol tracks. It subsequently identifies patterns and uses these insights to predict potential poaching hotspots. Rangers then prioritize their routes based on these predictions, substantially improving their response times and potentially saving countless lives.

9.4. AI in Species Counts and Assessments

Accurate species counting and population assessments are among the cornerstones of effective conservation programs. Traditionally, these processes are labor-intensive, time-consuming, and error-prone as they mostly rely on human observation. Here again, AI has come to the rescue.

For instance, Microsoft's AI for Earth initiative has proven to be revolutionary in this regard. Using machine learning models, it helps in interpreting aerial images to produce accurate species counts. This technological intervention has honed counting processes, helping track changes in population dynamics more quickly and accurately, enhancing our capacity to respond to any alarming shifts.

9.5. AI in Habitat & Biodiversity Monitoring

Another transformative application of AI technology in wildlife conservation has been in habitat and biodiversity monitoring. The Nature Conservancy has developed an AI system in collaboration with Google, aptly named "Soundscape." This project utilises Google's AI technology, studying sound data to monitor biodiversity in different ecosystems.

Unlike traditional monitoring methods, this approach mitigates the need for physical presence, hence limiting human interference in these sensitive ecosystems. Thus, AI in this context increases our awareness and understanding of these integral ecosystems, driving data-backed conservation strategies.

These success stories only offer a glimpse into the expansive potential benefits that AI and machine learning technologies bring to the table in wildlife conservation. The successful application of this transformative technology holds immense promise for the future of our planet, underscoring the fact that harmonizing technology with nature is not just doable or desirable — it is essential for the longevity of our rich and diverse ecosystems. AI, hence, unfolds as the synergistic link between human effort and technological advancement in the ceaseless pursuit of wildlife conservation.

Chapter 10. Ethical Considerations in AI-Driven Wildlife Management

The merging of AI with wildlife conservation efforts comes with the promise of remarkable advances. Despite the exciting potential, the amalgamation of such powerful technology with a complex, interconnected field like ecology necessitates a review of pertinent ethical issues. These range from decision transparency to possible disruptions in wildlife behavior, data privacy, and potential abuse or weaponization of the technology. It's crucial to thoughtfully traverse these ethical landscapes to ensure we balance the gains from AI with the considerations of the ecosystems and species we aim to protect.

10.1. Transparency in Decision Making

One of the defining features of AI and machine learning is their ability to 'learn' and adapt independently, leading to robust prediction models unparalleled by human analysts. However, often these algorithms function as black boxes. Insights from these models, while accurate, lack a clear storyline about how the results were derived. This raises ethical questions about decision transparency.

For instance, an AI system might suggest a plan of action to protect a certain species based on various factors. While potentially more accurate than human-based predictions, if this plan doesn't provide a clear 'how' and 'why', it might result in misunderstanding or misinformation. These worries underscore the importance of transparency in AI-driven conservation efforts.

Recently, there has been an emphasis on designing AI-based models that are not just accurate but also explainable. Developers are now working on what's known as 'Explainable AI' (XAI). Unlike conventional black box AI, XAI provides insights into its decision-making processes. By enhancing the transparency of AI implementations in wildlife management, we can help alleviate concerns related to decision ambiguity and improve trust in AI-guided conservation strategies.

10.2. Ethical Treatment of Animals

Wildlife management efforts often require extensive surveillance of animal populations. With AI-integrated tracking solutions, this surveillance is more effective than ever. However, AI's efficiency in tracking animals might inadvertently lead to intrusions into animals' lives, raising significant ethical concerns.

AI systems can track animals via GPS collars, drones, automated cameras, and more. While technologically impressive, these intrusive gadgets can cause animals stress, disrupt their daily routines, or even affect their social structures. There is a growing academic and societal concern that observing wildlife, when done without consideration for the well-being of animals under surveillance, is an infringement of their rights.

Given this, it's vital that the implementation of AI should maintain a balance between effectively monitoring wildlife and respecting their space and well-being, a consideration that extends beyond simple utilitarianism.

10.3. Data Privacy Concerns

Data privacy and security are crucial issues that arise in many spheres where AI is implemented, and wildlife conservation is no exception. With the large amount of highly revealing data gathered on animal behaviors, we might inadvertently endanger their habitats or routines if the data undergoes unauthorized access or misuse. For instance, poachers could potentially leverage such data to locate endangered animals.

In light of these risks, robust security protocols are a necessity in AI-driven wildlife management efforts. While sharing data can provide excellent insights for conservation researchers worldwide, the ethical obligation to protect the subjects of study—wildlife—must be given due consideration. Encryption, anonymization, and secure databasing are all tools that could be leveraged to secure wildlife data.

10.4. Possibility of Tech Abuse

The weaponization or abuse of technology is a significant concern with any advanced AI applications. In the context of wildlife conservation, the misuse of AI might come at a high cost to the animals and habitats.

For instance, certain AI applications can map out comprehensive topography of a specific area or track animal populations. These AI abilities could potentially be misused by illicit groups to exploit natural resources unlawfully or even to engage in geostrategic manipulation.

Recognizing these concerns, all stakeholders must work towards adopting legal and policy standards for the responsible use of AI, ensuring robust checks and balances to prevent the misuse of this technology in wildlife conservation.

10.5. Making AI Accessible

Finally, it is essential to focus on the equitable distribution of AI technology. Given the general expense of these technologies, there is a risk that only well-funded organizations in affluent countries will be able to deploy AI for conservation purposes. This runs the risk of taking advanced technological aids away from poorer, often biodiversity-rich regions that might need it the most.

Addressing this ethical concern involves driving costs down to make AI-powered tools more accessible. Open-source AI platforms, shared knowledge banks, and international collaborations could help to democratize AI technology for wildlife conservation.

In conclusion, while AI has immense potential to revolutionize wildlife conservation, ethical considerations must be at the heart of its employment. It's the role of policymakers, technologists, conservationists, and communities to work alongside each other, ensuring this technology is advanced and applied responsibly.

Chapter 11. Future Trends: The Evolution of AI in Wildlife Conservation and Management

The transformational wave of technology, particularly artificial intelligence and machine learning, is sweeping across the domain of wildlife conservation, mapping out promising trends for the future. Leveraging the potential of these advanced digital tools, researchers and conservationists can better protect ecosystems and manage biodiversity in our global struggle against environmental challenges.

11.1. Tracking and Monitoring Wildlife

One significant area where AI has proven beneficial is in the real-time tracking and monitoring of wildlife species. Traditional methods often include tagging or collaring the animals, which can be invasive and cause distress. Introducing AI into this field automates and simplifies the process, improving the effectiveness of these critical conservation tasks.

Machine learning algorithms, for example, are currently being trained to recognize and classify animal behavior based on accelerometry data collected from non-invasive tracking devices attached to the animal. These algorithms can identify normal behaviors and spatial patterns, assisting in the early detection of abnormal behaviors that might indicate disease or another threat to the animal's well-being.

Additionally, camera traps integrated with AI sensors can

automatically identify species, gender, and age, reducing the time it takes to process photographs manually. This allows researchers a more thorough understanding of species diversity, distribution, and behavior in a particular area.

11.2. Drone Technology in Wildlife Conservation

When combined with drones, AI technology creates excellent and non-invasive means for wildlife monitoring and data collection. Drones equipped with AI capabilities can survey large areas in short periods, providing conservationists with detailed, high-resolution imagery that can feed further AI models.

AI drones can identify, count, and monitor individual animals remotely, analyzing patterns in behavior and movement. This offers immense benefits for studying migration patterns or observing endangered species without disturbing them.

In the future, we may see drones going beyond simple reconnaissance. Some experimental projects are already aiming to develop drones that can plant trees or release beneficial organisms onto crops, demonstrating the potential for AI drones to contribute actively to conservation and restoration efforts.

11.3. AI and Citizen Science

Citizen science, where the public participates in data collection, is becoming an increasingly vital tool in conservation. AI can upgrade the contribution of these citizen scientists by providing them with AI-powered apps to accurately identify and log wildlife encounters accurately.

With AI tools, these records become more valuable and can provide real-time updates for species data. For example, the iNaturalist app uses machine learning to suggest identifications for organisms from photos uploaded by its users, improving data accuracy and user engagement.

This interaction between artificial intelligence and citizen science enhances mass-scale data collection, thereby fueling more research and conservation efforts.

11.4. Addressing Human-Wildlife Conflict

AI technology also has the potential to mitigate human-wildlife conflict, an enduring issue in conservation. By tracking and predicting animal movement in real-time, AI can send early warning alerts to communities living in close proximity to wildlife, preventing potential encounters.

Machine learning models can analyze the past interactions and movements of animals to predict their future behaviors accurately. This information, once shared with local communities, can help them take preventive measures to reduce conflicts with wildlife.

11.5. Challenges and Ethical Considerations

Despite the promising potential and strides made in integrating AI into wildlife conservation, several challenges and ethical considerations persist that require careful navigation.

The reliability of AI and machine learning greatly depends on the quality and quantity of the input data. However, there can be significant gaps in data, especially in the remote and hard-to-reach parts of the world.

The inherent bias in AI, stemming from its human creators, can lead to inaccuracies and unfair outcomes. Building ethical AI models that protect wildlife while ensuring fairness to local communities is an area where much work still needs to be done.

Moreover, despite AI's automation potential, skilled humans are still needed to train, troubleshoot, and update AI models, underscoring a crucial need for tech literacy in the conservation field.

In conclusion, the evolution of AI technology provides a wealth of opportunities for wildlife conservation and management. Notwithstanding the challenges, the intersection between technology and conservation holds significant potential. By leveraging AI's capabilities to improve tracking, monitoring, data collection, and engage citizen science, we are gearing up for a more sustainable future. Through persistence, collaboration, and innovative spirit, we can continue to forge the AI-enabled conservation strategies of tomorrow. Indeed, the blend of AI and wildlife management marks an intersection where the survival of the fittest meets survival by the smartest.